MW00412516

THE REVLON GIRL

by Neil Anthony Docking

SAMUEL FRENCH

samuelfrench.co.uk

THINKING ABOUT PERFORMING A SHOW?

There are thousands of plays and musicals available to perform from Samuel French right now, and applying for a licence is easier and more affordable than you might think

---

From classic plays to brand new musicals, from monologues to epic dramas, there are shows for everyone.

Plays and musicals are protected by copyright law so if you want to perform them, the first thing you'll need is a licence. This simple process helps support the playwright by ensuring they get paid for their work, and means that you'll have the documents you need to stage the show in public.

Not all our shows are available to perform all the time, so it's important to check and apply for a licence before you start rehearsals or commit to doing the show.

LEARN MORE & FIND THOUSANDS OF SHOWS

Browse our full range of plays and musicals and find out more about how to license a show

www.samuelfrench.co.uk/perform

Talk to the friendly experts in our Licensing team for advice on choosing a show, and help with licensing

plays@samuelfrench.co.uk   020 7387 9373

Acting Editions

BORN TO PERFORM

Playscripts designed from the ground up to work the way you do in rehearsal, performance and study

---

Larger, clearer text for easier reading

Wider margins for notes

Performance features such as character and props lists, sound and lighting cues, and more

---

+ CHOOSE A SIZE AND STYLE TO SUIT YOU

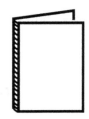

STANDARD EDITION

Our regular paperback book at our regular size

SPIRAL-BOUND EDITION

The same size as the Standard Edition, but with a sturdy, easy-to-fold, easy-to-hold spiral-bound spine

LARGE EDITION

A4 size and spiral bound, with larger text and a blank page for notes opposite every page of text. Perfect for technical and directing use

---

LEARN MORE | **samuelfrench.co.uk/actingeditions**

FIND PERFECT PLAYS TO PERFORM AT
www.samuelfrench.co.uk/perform

ABOUT THE AUTHOR

Neil Anthony Docking was born in South Wales and studied
music at the University of Westminster before finding work as
a writer in press, television, radio and film (credits include: *The
Guardian, Emmerdale, Casualty, Station Road, Nuts & Bolts,
TVCC, Without a Song or a Dance, Crossroads, The Throne
Room* and *Rain*). *The Revlon Girl* is his first play for theatre.

He is married to the actor/director Maxine Evans and lives in
London.

AUTHOR'S NOTE

The play's "encore" is traditionally used, first, to enable the cast to clear the stage (as if packing up at the end of the evening and returning the function room to its empty state) and, second, to give the audience a chance to recover from the intensity of the play before they leave.

For Maxine, for everything.

First presented as a short version in 2015 as part of a double bill staged at the Tristan Bates Theatre (Covent Garden). This version was first performed in 2017 at the Pontardawe Arts Centre just before its inclusion at the Edinburgh Fringe Festival (at the Assembly Roxy) and its subsequent London run at Park Theatre (Finsbury Park) featuring the following cast:

SIAN	Charlotte Gray
MARILYN/JACKIE	Michelle McTernan
REVLON	Antonia Kinlay
RONA	Bethan Thomas
JEAN	Zoë Harrison

Directed by	Maxine Evans
Lighting Design	Chris Barrett
Set Design	Eleri Lloyd
Special Technical Effects	Dan Travers
Original Music & Sound Design	Neil Anthony Docking

CHARACTERS
(in order of appearance)

SIAN – late twenties, bright, hopeful and eager to help, Sian is very much the instigator (and defender) of the evening's event and is desperate for it to go well.

REVLON – around the same age as Sian (if not younger) Revlon is smart, well-groomed, well-bred, trusting and clearly does not come from a Welsh working-class mining village.

MARILYN – early to mid-thirties, Marilyn is introverted, tense and fearful of change. Though outwardly simple, she is very focused.

RONA – early to mid-thirties, Rona is fiery, foul-mouthed and indomitable. She finds strength in rage, rejects authority and is easily set alight.

JEAN – early to mid-thirties, Jean is stately, conservative and sociable. Though she hails from the same background as Marilyn and Rona, Jean is now the wife of a respected church minister and therefore regards herself as a pillar of the community.

JACKIE (UNSEEN) – the hotel's part-time receptionist/ barmaid; helpful but inattentive.

SETTING

The action takes place in a function room above the Aberfan Hotel (a public house in the village) on a balmy, rainy evening in June 1967 – eight months after the disaster.

A NOTE ABOUT CASTING

The character ages – as specified in the text – reflect the likely ages of the real-life women at the heart of this story. However, for practical purposes, the important thing is that **MARILYN**, **RONA** and **JEAN** should be cast similarly in terms of age (as they were in school together) with **SIAN** appearing to be a few years younger; much closer to the age of **REVLON** who should appear to be the youngest of all.

Though based on actual events, *The Revlon Girl* is a work of dramatic fiction and any similarity to real persons is coincidental.

Excerpts from the 1960s advertising campaigns as seen in the text remain the property of Revlon Consumer Products Corporation and are reproduced under license.

Pre-set, dimly lit.

*We hear the sound of children playing. A school bell rings
and the children run obediently to their classrooms.
We settle on the sounds of an October day in a mining
village.*

*Then the stage darkens as, distantly, we hear an ominous
rumble; a deadly, unseen mass that's coming this way
and moving with alarming speed.*

*It builds to a terrifying roar as uprooted trees and heavy
debris crack and pound inside the thundering avalanche.
It can't be stopped. It can't be outrun. It's upon us...*

*Suddenly silence; darkness. We hear water trickling –
running freely – and then we hear the sound of rain...*

Fade up to:

The Aberfan Hotel – June 1967.

*Thunder announces the function room above the Aberfan
Hotel. It's early evening and rain falls heavily on the
roof. In the soft light we see water drip from a skylight
and down onto the floor of the empty room.*

*A silhouette of a woman appears at a doorway. She feels
for the light-switch and a bare bulb snaps on, revealing
SIAN (mid- to late twenties, bright, hopeful, eager).*

*She looks around the bare room and smiles. Then,
eagerly, she exits and returns with a table. Setting
it down carefully she takes her handbag and wet
plastic hat and places them on the table before
noticing the pool of water on the floor. She looks up*

at the leaking skylight and, with a groaning sigh, she heads back towards the door, and shouts downstairs...

SIAN Jackie?

No answer.

Jackie?

JACKIE *(offstage)* Yeah?

SIAN Is there a bucket or something up here I can use?

JACKIE *(offstage)* A what?

SIAN A bucket?

JACKIE *(offstage)* What do you want a bucket for?

SIAN To catch the drips from the – um – the thingy—

JACKIE *(offstage)* The what?

SIAN The skylight. Water's getting in again. It's all over the floor.

JACKIE *(offstage)* Must be from the skylight.

SIAN Yeah – is there a bucket?

JACKIE *(offstage)* If you want, there's a bucket in the cleaner's cupboard. Do you know where that is?

SIAN Yeah, I know.

SIAN *exits.*

JACKIE *(offstage)* It's out on the landing. On the right hand side, by the Ladies...

SIAN *(offstage)* Yeah, I know.

JACKIE *(offstage)* Only be careful when opening the door—

Sound of a crash as the contents of a broom cupboard tumble out onto the landing floor.

JACKIE *(offstage)* it might need a tidy.

Beat.

JACKIE *(offstage)* Did you find it?

SIAN *enters carrying a zinc bucket and mop.*

SIAN Yeah. Found it. Thanks.

SIAN *mops up the puddle and places the bucket underneath the skylight; catching each drip with a hollow clunk.*

SIAN *carries on mopping the floor around the bucket – her back to the door – and* REVLON *enters (early twenties, smart, well-bred, trusting), carrying a wet umbrella, handbag and vanity case.*

REVLON Hi!

SIAN *(jumping slightly)* Oh, hello.

REVLON Am I in the right place?

SIAN Yes. I think. Are you the Revlon lady?

REVLON Yes. Are you Audrey?

SIAN No, "Sian". I'm Sian. You know, "Sian"?

REVLON Of course – "Sian". Hi, Sian.

SIAN Hi. *(Then.)* We've got a leak!

REVLON I can see.

SIAN It's from the skylight. I thought they'd fixed it but they can't have. They can't have sealed it properly. But water will always find its way in somehow, won't it? All you need is a tiny— *(SIAN is staring and* REVLON *has noticed)* Sorry. I'm staring. I know. I'm a bugger for it. My husband's always telling me off for it. But I can't help it—

Then she says it.

You're very beautiful.

REVLON *blushes.*

But you don't need me to tell you that, but you are. Your hair, your make-up, your clothes – just beautiful.

REVLON Thank you. *(Then.)* Is there somewhere I can...? *(put my stuff down)*

SIAN Yes. Wait – wait!

SIAN *moves her belongings from the table and* REVLON *places hers down.*

REVLON Thank you. *(Then)* Is there anyone who can help me set up the room?

SIAN Yeah – me – I can. I'm "Sian". That's what I'm here for!

REVLON Oh right, oh yes, of course – "Sian". You're *Sian*.

SIAN Yes, I'm Sian. That's me.

REVLON *walks over to the other side of the room.*

REVLON So what do you think if we set up over here, Sian?

SIAN Up to you – whatever you think.

REVLON Yes, probably better over here.

SIAN *moves the table over.*

SIAN Oh yeah, much better over here. But we can do whatever. Everyone's just so pleased you could come.

REVLON Oh no, it's my pleasure. Well it's not my pleasure – I don't mean—

SIAN No, no, I know what you mean. So is that everything? Is that all the make-up?

REVLON No, there's more in the car. Actually, Sian...

Changing her mind, REVLON *moves back to the other side of the room; to the area under the bare light.*

...I think back here might be better after all.

SIAN *moves the table back to its original position.*

SIAN Oh yeah, much better back here. Did you say there's more in the car?

REVLON Yes.

SIAN Where's the car?

REVLON Outside.

SIAN Outside the front or outside the back?

REVLON Outside the front.

SIAN *(unsure)* The front – okay.

REVLON What's wrong with the front?

SIAN Nothing.

REVLON Should I move it?

SIAN Good God no. It's fine. You leave the car where it is. *(then)* Nobody spoke to you though, did they?

REVLON No. *(then)* Yes! The woman downstairs.

SIAN Jackie?

> REVLON *shrugs – no idea.*
>
> Oh Jackie's okay. She's fine. Jackie is fine. You leave the car where it is. *(then)* But if anyone asks you, you're from the W.I., giving a talk on poetry or something. Is that okay?

REVLON *(no idea why but...)* Yes...

> SIAN *smiles at* REVLON *and exits.*
>
> *Pause.*
>
> *Within a few moments,* SIAN *returns with a "make-up chair" (a high bar stool/chair).*

SIAN They said you might need one of these.

REVLON That's perfect!

SIAN So you've spoken to Audrey?

REVLON No, not yet. My boss has.

SIAN Okay.

> **SIAN** *exits again, leaving* **REVLON** *to wonder if she's coming back.*
>
> *Within moments,* **SIAN** *returns – now carrying a couple of folding chairs from the landing. She begins to set them out.*

Well, Audrey's lovely – really lovely.

REVLON Will she be coming tonight?

SIAN Oh yes, she'll be here now any minute; she's probably been held up, that's all. She spends a lot of time with the bereaved families, you know? The mothers especially. I honestly don't know how some of them would have coped without her—

> *Sound of a door banging out on the landing.*

Hello?

> *No answer.*

Hello?!

> *Nobody there.*

Yes, so that's where she'll be – with the mothers. The men, they don't – well, you know how men are.

REVLON Actually, can I ask you something, Sian?

SIAN Yes, luv?

REVLON The ladies that are coming tonight? Are they all...

> *She's unsure how to word it.*

SIAN Are they all what?

REVLON Are they all...? Did they all have...?

> **SIAN** *helps her.*

SIAN ...children in the school?

REVLON Yes.

SIAN Yes.

REVLON *was afraid of that.*

REVLON And how many...?

SIAN Died in the school? One hundred and nine. Plus the teachers of course. There were five of them – all buried with their kids. Youngest was seven; eldest was ten. The others were either walking to school or killed in their houses. It happened so quickly you see, nobody had a chance to get out. And there was no warning. So the final count was: one hundred and sixteen children and twenty-eight adults in all.

REVLON Sorry, I meant...how many mothers will be coming tonight?

SIAN *(laughing)* Oh, sorry luv, I didn't realise. I'm so dozy sometimes – it's like I'm on another planet. Um – I don't know. We never know. Sometimes it's quite a few. Sometimes it's hardly any.

SIAN *exits and returns with more chairs.*

They come when they feel up to it. If they want to have a chat or talk about what happened – you know? But to be honest, with a lot of them I still think it's sinking in. But then it's so much to take in, isn't it? It's so unbelievable – especially for a tiny village like this. I've lived here my whole life. I grew up here, I went to the same school, my son Paul went there – it's unbelievable.

SIAN *is already heading out to fetch more chairs.*

REVLON At least he was one of the lucky ones.

SIAN Oh no, he died too.

A moment. Then, SIAN *exits.* REVLON *waits – searching for something to say to* SIAN *when she returns.* SIAN *enters, again with some chairs.*

Yeah, he was in Mr Jones's class. Whole classroom filled up with slurry in seconds. All the children died. And Mr Jones too, of course.

SIAN *pauses; the raw emotion catching her a little by surprise. She contains it well but* REVLON *sees it (though can do little to help).* SIAN, *however, won't be beaten and she recovers herself for the sake of* REVLON *and the evening ahead.*

Now, is there anything else you need before we get the rest of your stuff in from the car?

REVLON *(nervously)* A drink, maybe?

SIAN Ohh, wouldn't that be nice? Tell you what, I'll nip down the bar in a sec; ask them to put the kettle on.

She winks and turns to exit. In the doorway is MARILYN *(mid-thirties, introverted, tense, outwardly simple but very focused).*

Well good heavens – look what the cat dragged in...

MARILYN *– seeing* REVLON *and clearly uncomfortable around strangers – comes no further.*

Was that you just then?

MARILYN *nods, but stays near the door.*

Well come in, luv. Don't be shy. This is the lady from Revlon. Come to talk to us. Doesn't she look lovely? Isn't she gorgeous? She's come all the way from...

REVLON Bristol.

SIAN *(to* MARILYN*)* Bristol... *(suddenly to* REVLON*)* Bristol?! Bloody heck! Sorry, shouldn't swear. My husband hates it when I swear.

REVLON Is this Audrey?

SIAN No – this is Marilyn.

REVLON Hello.

> **MARILYN** *replies with a brief, nervous smile.*

SIAN Marilyn doesn't come very often, do you, darling? She doesn't like leaving the house much these days, so you're really honoured.

MARILYN *(noticing the skylight)* There's water coming in.

SIAN Yeah I know, I've told them.

MARILYN And there's a car parked outside.

SIAN Yes darling, I know, we're going to say she's from the W.I.

MARILYN Have you heard the rumour?

SIAN No darling, what rumour?

MARILYN About the children being in assembly?

SIAN No darling, I don't think they were.

MARILYN Well that's what people are saying.

SIAN What people?

MARILYN People. Is that right?

SIAN No darling – now look, we need to get set up here. We need some more chairs from the landing; there's stuff to come in from the car... *(then remembering, at* **REVLON***)* Oh! And we're gasping for a cup of tea!

> *She exits. Pause.*

MARILYN *(to* **REVLON***)* Have you heard anything about the children being in assembly?

REVLON No. I'm not from the area so—

MARILYN Because that's not what they said at the inquest. It's different. They're saying now that the children were

in assembly when the tip came down. Is that right? Have
you heard that?

REVLON No, I'm not from the area. I wouldn't know.

Pause. **MARILYN** *fixes on* **REVLON***; drips beat relentlessly
into the bucket.*

MARILYN It's raining again.

REVLON *nods, unsettled – doubts about the evening are
now beginning to creep in. Thankfully,* **SIAN** *returns
with more chairs (***REVLON** *begins to unpack make-up
products from her case and place them on the small
table).*

SIAN How are you sleeping now, Marilyn?

MARILYN Not so good when the weather's like this.

SIAN No, I know. Grab a couple of these, will you?

MARILYN What if they were singing in assembly?

SIAN No darling, they weren't in assembly. We know they weren't.
They were in their classrooms. We know that. Don't we?

MARILYN *nods. She does know.*

MARILYN Did I show you Glynis's drawing?

MARILYN *produces a piece of well-worn and folded cartridge
paper.*

SIAN Yes darling, you did. It's very good.

(*To* **REVLON***)* Marilyn's daughter was a fantastic artist.
Wasn't she, Marilyn? And Annette, her other daughter?
What a swimmer!

MARILYN *is about to show* **REVLON** *the drawing when*
SIAN *routinely and gently pushes it away.*

Marilyn! Chairs.

MARILYN *does what she's told.*

SIAN *(back to* **REVLON***)* Yeah – like a dolphin she was. So: do you want to get the rest of your stuff in from the car?

Now panic sets in for **REVLON** *as she sees a withdrawn, timid* **MARILYN** *struggle with a chair.*

REVLON How long do you think Audrey's going to be?

SIAN Why, what's wrong?

REVLON *(looking at* **MARILYN***)* Nothing.

SIAN turns to see that **MARILYN** *has the chair the wrong way around.*

SIAN Oh no, they're not all like Marilyn.

(Beat)

They're much more outgoing. And they're all really excited. Have your tea now and wait for Audrey – she'll explain everything. But honestly – everyone round here is so lovely: so warm, so friendly, so welcoming—

RONA *(offstage)* WHAT A LOAD OF SHIT! What a load of fucking shit!!!

RONA enters. (Mid-thirties, fiery, indomitable, finds strength in rage)

I've heard some bollocks since that bastard came down: that "the tips were safe"; "nobody knew there was a stream"; "we ought to have a committee", well let me tell you what that committee wants to do with a million quid— *(then)* Who's this?

SIAN This—

RONA This is the Revlon Girl.

SIAN Yes.

REVLON *(to* **SIAN***)* This isn't Audrey, is it?

RONA Fuck no!

Beat.

...but I'll be talking to her too when she gets here; you've got a leak in the ceiling, Sian!

SIAN I know.

RONA So yeah – listen to this – they want to build a swimming pool! A fucking swimming pool!

SIAN Rona – please – can you not swear?

RONA Oh fuck off, Sian. We're in a pub, not a church. Is Jean here?

SIAN No.

RONA Is she coming?

SIAN I should think so.

RONA She'd better. I want to know what Billy has to say. A swimming pool – what's the fucking point of a swimming pool?! *(seeing* MARILYN*)* Good God – what are you doing here?

MARILYN I'm not stopping. I'm going home.

SIAN No darling, you're staying. Rona, tell her.

RONA Marilyn, go home!

SIAN Rona!

RONA She doesn't want to stay.

SIAN Yes she does. Please Marilyn – just for a while – we'll be having a cup of tea now in a minute.

RONA Aye, alright then, if you're making – just a drop of milk for me. And hey – have you seen? Brand new Zodiac parked right out the front. Right-out-in-the-fucking-*street*! Makes you sick, people throwing their money around like that. Whose is it? Does anyone know?

Pause. **REVLON** *sheepishly raises a hand.*

Lovely cars aren't they? *(To* **SIAN***)* She's not leaving it out there, is she?

SIAN We're going to say she's from the W.I.

They look at the stylish **REVLON***...*

Or maybe the Red Cross would be better?

RONA Oh yeah Red Cross: nobody'll suspect a fucking thing.

MARILYN *(To* **RONA***)* Have you heard the rumour?

RONA No.

(To **REVLON***)* Husband's car is it?

REVLON No, no. It's mine.

MARILYN There's a rumour about the children being in assembly.

RONA *(dismissive)* Is there?

MARILYN Is that right?

RONA No, Marilyn – they didn't have assembly on Fridays.

MARILYN *ponders this.* **RONA** *sidles up to* **REVLON***.*

Hasn't tried to put you in touch with the spirit world yet, has she? *(She hasn't)* Stick around.

RONA *takes one of* **REVLON***'s tissues and blows her nose forcefully into it. Then, once finished, she deposits the used tissue on* **REVLON***'s table before taking a fresh one and returning to her seat.*

SIAN I'm so sorry about the swearing.

REVLON *gingerly lifts the used tissue to throw it away.*

REVLON Don't worry, I feel like doing some myself.

JEAN *enters. (Mid-thirties, stately, conservative, sociable)* **REVLON** *thinks this is the aforementioned "***AUDREY***".*

SIAN *(relieved)* Oh, thank god.

JEAN I know. I'm sorry. I got held up.

REVLON Oh hello, I'm—

JEAN I know who you are – you're the lady from Revlon.

REVLON Yes. Is there somewhere we could have a quick chat?

JEAN Of course.

RONA Woah – hang on – I've been waiting to talk to this one.

REVLON Please – it'll only take a minute...

> **JEAN** *takes* **REVLON** *to one side (the others watch and try to listen).*

REVLON *(confidentially to* **JEAN***)* I know you spoke to my boss and she was keen to help – as was I; in fact I volunteered – but the thing is, after meeting some of the ladies, I'm starting to think that—

(Then)

You're not Audrey are you?

JEAN No, I'm Jean.

REVLON Jean?

JEAN Yes Jean.

REVLON *(to* **SIAN***)* Not Audrey?

SIAN No, Jean.

REVLON "Jean".

JEAN Jean.

REVLON Jean?

JEAN Yes, Jean.

REVLON *Not* Audrey?

RONA NO SHE'S FUCKING JEAN!

REVLON Nice to meet you Jean.

JEAN It's nice to meet you too. Anyone know whose car that is parked out the front?

REVLON *grabs her handbag and heads for the door.*

SIAN Where're you going?

REVLON To move my car.

SIAN No, don't – it's fine. *(to the others)* I told her it was fine.

JEAN But what if someone should see it?

SIAN Then we'll say she's from the W.I.

RONA What happened to the Red Cross?

JEAN I don't think people from the Red Cross look like that.

Everyone now looks again at the stylish REVLON.

SIAN Salvation Army then?!

REVLON Okay, can I ask something? Why can't people know who I am or where I'm from?

JEAN *(to* SIAN*)* Hasn't she spoken to Audrey?

REVLON *hasn't. A pause.* SIAN *realises that the others expect her to explain.*

SIAN Since the disaster we've all kind of...forgotten about ourselves. You know, the way we look? And some of us thought it would be a nice idea to have someone like you to come along and give us a talk on beauty tips – a demonstration – that's all. But the thing is – given what's happened – some people might think it's wrong for us to worry about the way we look. They might think it's stupid.

RONA It is.

REVLON No it isn't. I don't think so.

RONA Course you don't – you've got a brand-new Zodiac parked out the front.

SIAN Rona!

RONA What? I'm just saying, it must pay well.

JEAN *sees* MARILYN.

JEAN Hello Marilyn – how have you been?

MARILYN *avoids eye contact. Bad blood clearly.* SIAN – *ever the diplomat – steps in.*

SIAN Marilyn's heard a rumour about the children being in assembly.

JEAN Yes, I heard that one too.

RONA Forget that shit – what's all this about a swimming pool?

JEAN Oh God. I don't know anything about it.

RONA Your husband sits on the Disaster Fund committee and you don't know anything about it?

JEAN No.

RONA Nothing?

JEAN No, not really. *(then)* What time are we starting?

SIAN When everyone's here.

RONA "Not really"? What does "not really" mean?

JEAN It's just an idea, that's all I know.

(to SIAN*)* Are we having a preview?

SIAN *(to* REVLON*)* Ooh, can we?

RONA An idea?

JEAN Yes.

RONA Just an idea?

JEAN Yes.

RONA Well you can tell them from me that it's a stupid idea.

JEAN There's a leak in this ceiling, Sian.

SIAN I know.

RONA Did you hear me?

SIAN It's coming from the skylight.

RONA Did you hear me?

JEAN I did. I heard you.

RONA A stupid fucking idea.

JEAN Yes. Thank you, Rona. I'll tell them.

SIAN I thought they'd fixed it.

RONA Cos I don't know who they think is going to swim in this
pool – all the kids are dead!

Pause. A big one. Even **RONA** *can't quite believe what
she's said.*

REVLON Sorry, excuse me a minute.

REVLON *takes her bag and exits.* **SIAN** *and* **JEAN** *follow,*
SIAN *venturing out onto the landing while* **JEAN** *turns
to shoot an admonishing look at* **RONA**.

RONA *knows she's wrong but is unrepentant. She turns
away, leaving* **JEAN** *to fume for a few moments – clearly
embarrassed by the undignified show* **REVLON** *has just
witnessed. Calming slightly,* **JEAN** *finds herself near*
MARILYN. *Though attempting to build a bridge between
them,* **JEAN** *retains her detached and superior tone.*

JEAN I was up the cemetery earlier. Saw Ken.

MARILYN He goes up there.

JEAN I helped him clear the dead flowers from the girls' grave.
I put some fresh ones down—

MARILYN *doesn't want to hear it.*

Why don't you come to church again this Sunday? Listen to Billy speak?

MARILYN *almost recoils and turns away.*

RONA Leave her alone, Jean.

JEAN *does so (for now).* **SIAN** *returns, voice lowered.*

SIAN She's on the phone. I think she's talking to her boss. You don't think she's trying to back out of it, do you?

RONA Good God, no – who'd want to miss all this?

SIAN I think we've upset her.

JEAN She's probably just checking in or something.

RONA Oh Christ – who cares – what's she doing here anyway? A girl like that.

JEAN She told me she volunteered.

RONA Oh well, if she told you—

SIAN Well she can't back out now! She can't—

Shush! **REVLON** *is returning – head down – carrying another vanity case.*

Everything okay?

REVLON *(overcompensating)* Fine. Just went to move the car.

SIAN There was no need to do that.

REVLON It's fine.

JEAN *(pointing at the vanity case)* And Sian would have brought that in for you.

REVLON Honestly – it's fine.

Pause. Something's happened, clearly.

SIAN Jean – didn't you ask about a preview or something?

JEAN I just thought it'd be nice to see before everyone else gets here.

SIAN *(delighted, to* REVLON*)* Oh yes – what do you think?

REVLON A preview. Okay.

SIAN Oh brilliant! Brilliant, brilliant, brilliant. I can't wait.

RONA Aye, go on then – before the crowds get here.

REVLON Crowds?

SIAN No not crowds. She doesn't mean crowds.

JEAN *(unbuttoning her coat)* No, and – if there are – we'll have had a practice run first. And how bad can it be anyway? As I say to people: "In God I trust and am not afraid; for what can mere mortals do to me?"

JEAN takes off her coat and we see she's around eight months pregnant.

REVLON, surprised, is about to congratulate JEAN when SIAN, with a small but clear gesture, urges REVLON not to say anything. REVLON complies (but doesn't know why). All of which has gone unnoticed by JEAN who, by now, has found a seat and is placing her coat over the back of a chair.

She looks up and assumes mistakenly that they are waiting for her (and is almost delighted to think that the others can't begin until she's ready).

So sorry – are you waiting for me?

Almost regally, she sits.

Ready now.

A few beats. REVLON checks her notes.

REVLON Okay...well usually I start by saying:
Good evening ladies and welcome to—

RONA Speak up, Revlon – they'll be standing all the way to the back.

REVLON shudders a little at the thought. SIAN glares at RONA who feigns innocence. REVLON steels herself for another try.

REVLON *(a little louder)* Good evening ladies and welcome to the world of Revlon: where every woman deserves to look and feel beautiful.

Getting into her stride a little.

We have some fabulous products to show you today – sorry, tonight – and some truly life-changing make-up and breath-taking colours that will in an instant bring *new life* to your skin. Whether you're a career girl or a busy mum... *(A moment, she begins to falter)* We'll sweep away those deep worry-lines, banish those dull, tired eyes and give your skin a fresh, born again... I'm sorry.

Emotion suddenly overwhelms REVLON and she turns away from them, trying to hide her tears.

JEAN What's the matter?

REVLON Do you think I could have a glass of water?

SIAN Would you prefer a cup of tea?

REVLON Water'll be fine.

SIAN *(to RONA)* See? We did upset her!

SIAN scurries off for water.

REVLON I just need a tissue...

Everyone has one and they each offer theirs simultaneously. REVLON has one in her case. SIAN returns with a glass of water for REVLON.

JEAN Come on now, tell us what's wrong.

RONA Got an eyelash stuck, have you luv?

SIAN She's had a very long drive. (*mouths "from Bristol"*)

JEAN *is impressed and mouths it back.* MARILYN *is curious while* RONA*'s eyes roll.*

REVLON It's not that.

SIAN What then?

REVLON (*to* SIAN) Can you pass me that mirror please?

SIAN (*handing her the mirror*) You look fine – doesn't she?

REVLON I'm sorry. It's stupid. I'm being stupid – considering what you all went through. It was just so terrible.

RONA We know luv, we were there.

JEAN What's wrong with you?

RONA What? I'm trying to cheer her up!

REVLON I'm sorry. It won't happen again. But you feel so helpless, don't you? I sent money by the way. I did. Not much, but I did.

SIAN Oh that was kind. Wasn't that kind?

RONA Very kind. Why the hell didn't she say something sooner?

A pause as REVLON *composes herself.*

SIAN Are you okay now?

REVLON (*gratefully*) Yes, thank you.

Pause. REVLON *looks at the ladies. They all wait expectantly.*

You want me to carry on?

SIAN Good God yeah, I was loving that!

JEAN Me too. It was really good. Wasn't it good?

RONA Up until the point you started crying I couldn't fault it.

SIAN That bit about every woman deserving to be beautiful – wasn't that good?

JEAN agrees. RONA nods. Then:

MARILYN Yes, that was good.

This surprises everyone. Slowly they all turn to look at MARILYN who darts back a look that says, "What? What did I say?".

REVLON Well, okay then. Well – what I usually ask for now is a volunteer.

SIAN raises her hand.

SIAN Oh!

RONA Hold your horses – I was first!

RONA is already up, pushing SIAN's hand down, and takes her place in the make-up chair.

JEAN What a surprise.

RONA Shurrup, don't care.

JEAN It's not like Rona to jump a queue, is it girls?

MARILYN She does that. She does that in the post office.

This is true enough and the women taunt RONA with a knowing laugh.

RONA If people are happy to wait in line then that's up to them. I won't be queuing for anything ever again, I can tell you that.

REVLON Don't worry, Sian, we'll get to you.

RONA Yeah – see Sian – we'll get to you.

REVLON So, Rona – could you tell us about your beauty regime?

A beat.

RONA My what?

REVLON Your beauty regime – what you do to keep yourself looking young.

JEAN Whatever it is, it isn't enough.

RONA Hey!

REVLON Now, I assume you cleanse every day?

RONA *(unsure)* I do...

> **RONA** *desperately looks at* **SIAN** *for help.*

SIAN She's asking you if you wash.

RONA I wash!

> *(then to* **REVLON***)* My face, you mean?

REVLON Absolutely. But it's much more than that – the key to any beauty regime starts with a "cleanse, tone and moisturise".

> **REVLON** *prepares to cleanse.* **JEAN** *raises her hand.*

JEAN I have a question.

REVLON Yes.

JEAN Who does the Queen's make-up?

REVLON I don't know.

SIAN *(hand up)* She'd have her own make-up person, wouldn't she?

REVLON I expect so.

SIAN Oh, wouldn't that be nice?

JEAN I don't think she wears a lot of make-up though, does she? Well she didn't on the day she came anyway.

Not that I could see and I was standing right next to her practically. It was so good of her to come and walk around the site; it was so filthy but she didn't care. And when she talked to some of the mothers, mother to mother, it was heartbreaking. I didn't get to meet her myself but I was this close to her. And I have to say her skin was radiant.

RONA   Course it was – woman doesn't wash a dish!

JEAN   What's that supposed to mean?

RONA   Means the woman never bends down. I don't think she knows what her knees look like.

JEAN   Just because she doesn't scrub her own floors doesn't mean she doesn't work. It's quite a strain meeting people like that you know – trying to lift their spirits. And I think it did lift their spirits. It was good for the people to see her that day.

RONA   Yeah and it was good for her to see where she gets her coal.

REVLON   So first we apply the cream cleanser evenly. Making sure we cleanse the entire face using sideways strokes, working the cleanser. How's that?

RONA   Cold. *(then)* Nice though.

JEAN, SIAN and MARILYN are entranced.

REVLON   Okay, so now we take the cleanser off with a little cotton wool. And then – again with cotton wool – we will tone the skin, closing all those pores using our universal toning lotion.

Everyone's breathing is slower and deeper. The atmosphere is calm.

(removing the cleanser) It's very calming, isn't it?

SIAN/JEAN/MARILYN   *(agreeing)* Mmm.

They continue watching REVLON *calmly cleansing* RONA's *face (even she has closed her eyes now). Pause. It's peaceful, until...*

RONA   So how much money did you give?

An audible groan from the others.

No, come on. How much money did you give to the disaster fund?

REVLON I don't remember.

RONA Fair enough, but how much?

REVLON Six shillings.

> **RONA** *is mildly insulted.*

It was all I could spare that week.

> **RONA** *seems satisfied momentarily and* **REVLON** *is relieved to get back to cleansing and toning.*

RONA So if I was to ask you how you'd feel about your "six shillings" going towards a swimming pool, what would you say?

JEAN Look, it's just one idea. There's a whole load of ideas. There's talk of having a memorial, a—

RONA A memorial?!

JEAN Yes.

SIAN Are we toning now? Is this toner?

RONA What do we want a memorial for? If anyone wants a memorial, just look at the six tips left on the mountain. Leave them up there, I say.

MARILYN They're not going to do that, are they?

JEAN No, they're not.

RONA Well they look like they're still there to me.

REVLON Okay – so now we've toned, we moisturise...

MARILYN They can't leave the tips there – they can't.

SIAN They won't, Marilyn, they won't.

JEAN *(to* **RONA***)* So what do you think we should do with the money?

RONA Share it out. Share it out between us.

JEAN They can't, Rona, and you know it.

RONA Why not?

JEAN It's too much money.

RONA Too much money? Too much money?! Too much for
who – the little people?

JEAN I didn't say that.

SIAN She didn't, Rona, she didn't.

RONA That's what she meant! And can you believe this is one
of the little people talking. No matter what she thinks of
herself, no matter how many committees she sits on, she's
still one of the little people.

JEAN What I meant was – that amount of money can go and
benefit the whole community.

RONA With what – a swimming pool?

JEAN Yes. Possibly.

RONA See, this is what happens when they elect people like
her husband. He just does what he's told. Hasn't learned
his lesson yet. And do you know, there isn't one woman
from the village on that committee. Not one. Good enough
to be nominated but that's it. Makes you sick. This is why
I don't vote!

REVLON Oh, you must vote.

RONA What?

REVLON You must vote. It's very important. Particularly for
women.

RONA (playing dumb) Why's that then?

REVLON Because we had to fight for it.

RONA You're kidding me? I didn't know that. Marilyn, did you
know that? Remind me – what were we doing that day?

REVLON Oh no, I know, of course – actually it was my mother who said it.

SIAN *(hand in the air)* I have another question.

RONA So what do you think?

REVLON About what?

RONA About this money being shared out.

REVLON Oh, I don't know.

JEAN I think Sian has a question?

RONA Hold up – I want to know what she thinks. She gave us six whole shillings, so she has a say. I know – let's pretend she has a vote!

JEAN Nobody has a vote, Rona.

RONA No, I know.

(to REVLON*)* So – what do you think?

REVLON Well – alright, yes – if that's how it's needed.

RONA Hallelujah! "If that's how it's needed" – and people need it.

JEAN What for? We've all had money.

RONA Are you serious? Are you seriously fucking serious? "We've all had money" – Jesus!

(to REVLON*)* Do you know how much money we got? A few thousand. And that was from donations, not the Coal Board – and it was their fault! All they would pay out was five hundred pounds. That's a lot for my little boy, isn't it? Five hundred quid. And they did that when they were still lying about the stream underneath the tip.

MARILYN They knew – there were warnings.

RONA That's right – there were. But don't get your drawing out just yet okay, Marilyn?

JEAN Let's leave it: we've asked this lady here to give a talk and the last thing anyone wants to see is us airing our dirty washing.

RONA Fuck it – I don't care.

JEAN Well I do! And there's been enough of it in the papers.

(explaining to **REVLON***)* What everyone forgets is that when something like this happens, suddenly – without warning – it takes its toll.

MARILYN There were warnings.

JEAN No, I know – I mean out of the blue.

RONA What she means, Marilyn, is that it was an Act of God.

JEAN I didn't mean that and you know it.

RONA And get this – some people whose child wasn't killed could get more – they got something if they lost their house, or their stuff, or if their child was injured – or wasn't injured – it was like a one arm bandit. Just get the right combination and you hit the fucking jackpot!

SIAN Do you have to swear like that?

RONA Yes, I fucking do, because children are dead and she's talking about fucking swimming pools.

MARILYN We were warned: and Glynis drew this picture—

RONA We know, Marilyn, we've all seen it.

SIAN It's just a drawing, darling.

MARILYN No, it's not. I asked the medium about it and she said it was a premonition.

RONA Oh fuck, here we go. Everyone join hands!

MARILYN IT WAS A WARNING!! THEY WERE ALL WARNINGS. BUT *NOBODY WAS LISTENING*!!!

Pause. Another wound opens. **RONA** *knows it's gone too far (again). The mood darkens.*

REVLON *(to* **RONA***).* Okay, that's you done.

RONA Thank you. Feels nice.

> **RONA** *returns to her seat, unbowed.*

REVLON Maybe Marilyn would like to go next?

> **SIAN** *is next, but she makes way.*

> What do you say, Marilyn? Maybe we can show everyone how we get rid of dark circles under the eyes – that okay?

> **MARILYN** *nods and, almost defiantly, takes the make-up chair.*

MARILYN There were warnings. There was plenty.

REVLON Do you mind taking off your glasses? Looks to me like you have a little trouble sleeping.

MARILYN I'm on tablets. But I don't take them when it rains. It's too dangerous.

SIAN She's afraid that the other tips will come down. It had rained a lot in the weeks before the slip.

REVLON Well a little bit of concealer will brighten and smooth away those fine lines.

MARILYN Ever since they put the tips up there, there were warnings.

REVLON Look up for me?

> **REVLON** *applies concealer under* **MARILYN***'s eyes.*

MARILYN They said they didn't know they were tipping on a stream but they knew. They said at the inquest you can't tip muck on a stream – but they knew. Her brother knew but they kept on tipping.

> *She means* **JEAN***.*

JEAN John didn't know – none of them did. They were told where to tip, that was their job.

MARILYN But they shouldn't have tipped on a stream.

RONA Come on, Marilyn – she's right, they didn't know. Not like that.

MARILYN I heard them say on the television that they knew it was there.

RONA Yeah, but that was the Chargehand mouthing off in front of the cameras – but still—

JEAN You had no right to say what you said to my brother, Marilyn – no right.

MARILYN Everyone knew the tip was slipping. It had slipped before. The men knew, the council knew – they wrote letters to the Coal Board. I saw them all at the inquest. And then there was the petition from the Headmistress. She complained about the flooding but she was ignored.

REVLON That must be awful for her.

MARILYN She's dead now – she died in the school. No one wanted to know, not the council, not the Coal Board, not even the union. Not anyone. And still they kept on tipping.

JEAN You still had no right, Marilyn – my brother was just doing his job.

MARILYN But if he had stopped, no one would have died.

JEAN But John wasn't a *murderer*.

MARILYN Your brother worked on the tips. He built the tip that killed my girls.

JEAN And your husband dug the coal that made those tips. If my brother's a murderer, then what does that make your husband?

SIAN *quickly jumps in between them.*

SIAN Who wants a cup of tea?

A moment. Tempers are very high.

JEAN I'll make it.

JEAN *exits.*

RONA I bet you're glad you stuck around, eh, Revlon?

MARILYN And see, Glynis drew this picture; the night before she died: it shows you the tips and she wrote "The End" at the top. If it had happened the day after, no one would have died. If it had happened the following week it was half term – or if they'd been in assembly then maybe—

She breaks down.

REVLON I know. I read it in the newspapers. I saw it on the television.

MARILYN You saw it on the television?

REVLON Yes.

RONA A television and a Zodiac – no wonder she could only afford six shillings.

RONA *exits.*

MARILYN What did you see? Did you see me?

REVLON I don't think so. I can't remember.

MARILYN Because I wasn't right that day. I heard the tip coming down and I came out and saw it had come all the way down the mountain. I ran towards the school and saw all the houses on Moy Road were knocked down and that the school had been buried. I ran back home – just in case the girls had got out and were waiting for me. I called Ken at the colliery and he came with the other men. And I waited. I waited on my doorstep and watched as the people came to help. And then the reporters – they saw me – and they asked me if I had children in the school. I said I did. And then they asked me how I felt. What are you supposed to say to that?

REVLON I don't know – it's a stupid question.

RONA *re-enters and takes her seat.*

MARILYN And then came the sightseers – who came to look and stare and wait as the children got dug out. And the men: they found a boy and a girl near to each other. And the sightseers – who were standing on a bank of coal waste – they shoved forward to have a look – and it dislodged the bank – and the boy and girl were buried again. And they're still coming, those *people*. I can see them from my window, pulling up in their cars; getting out and looking where the school used to be. Then looking back up at the mountain at the tips.

RONA Let 'em come, I say. Send them up the tips and charge them a guinea for a bucket of slag; that'll get 'em cleared quick enough.

No laugh.

No? Please yourselves.

MARILYN Everyone knew. Everyone...

Pause. **REVLON** *hands* **MARILYN** *a mirror. She looks at herself and then, unable to stand what she sees, rubs off the concealer underneath her eyes.*

SIAN No, don't rub it off – you look so much better.

MARILYN I don't want to look better.

MARILYN *re-takes her seat as thunder heralds a spell of heavier rain.*

Pause. **REVLON** *turns back to her vanity case, replacing the concealer and rearranging some eyeshadows.*

SIAN *manages to catch* **REVLON***'s eye.*

SIAN Going well, isn't it?

Beat. **REVLON** *can't help but smile.*

Are those eyeshadows?

REVLON Yes.

SIAN Can I have a look?

REVLON Of course you can.

RONA Has anyone got any fags?

REVLON I don't smoke.

RONA Marilyn, have you got any fags? *(then)* Marilyn!

>   **MARILYN** *looks up.*

Have you got any fags?

MARILYN I've only got the one.

RONA That's alright, I only want the one.

JEAN *(offstage)* Sian?

SIAN Yeah.

JEAN *(offstage)* Give me a hand with these, will you?

SIAN Oh, yeah – sorry.

>   **SIAN** *goes to help* **JEAN** *and returns with the tea on a tray.*

JEAN It's starting to come down again out there – don't know how many women will come if it's raining.

MARILYN I should go home. Ken will be worrying where I am.

RONA Oh, sit down – Ken's not there – he's afternoons.

>   **SIAN** *places the tea tray down for* **JEAN** *and returns to the make-up chair.*

SIAN Yeah, Marilyn, I won't be seeing David until ten.

JEAN Have your tea. I made one for you.

RONA Yeah – have your tea – have a *fag!*

MARILYN I don't want one.

SIAN Why don't you wait until the rain stops? No sense going out in this.

The sound of heavy rain hitting the skylight convinces MARILYN *that she is right.*

JEAN *offers* MARILYN *a cup of tea once more.*

MARILYN No, thank you.

JEAN Please yourself.

JEAN *sees that* SIAN *is in the make-up chair and that* REVLON *is presenting her with eyeshadows.*

(miffed) Oh, have we started again?

REVLON No, we're just looking at some colours.

RONA Hang on: David's days, isn't he?

SIAN Overtime.

RONA Getting the money in – good boy.

SIAN No, he likes doing it. Says it helps him to think.

RONA Think? What the hell has he got to think about?

Beat.

SIAN *(to* REVLON*)* What does your husband do?

REVLON I'm not married.

SIAN *(commiserating)* Aw.

REVLON I was. Just not anymore.

JEAN *and* RONA *exchange a judgemental look ("divorce").*

SIAN *(understanding)* Oh.

(Then) I bet you're not short of offers though.

REVLON Not as many as I'd like.

They giggle.

JEAN *(disapproving but smiling)* Any children?

REVLON No.

REVLON *and* SIAN *skulk a little – almost like schoolgirls.*

RONA *(to* MARILYN*)* If I give you two back, will you give me that fag?

MARILYN No.

RONA I'll give you three then? Fuck, no – I'm not giving you three.

JEAN Have one of mine.

RONA Don't like yours – they give me a sore throat.

JEAN They most certainly do not.

MARILYN *(pointing at the skylight)* Water's really coming in now.

SIAN S'okay, Marilyn, someone will see to it now.

JEAN But they do know about it, don't they, Sian?

SIAN Oh yes, they know.

REVLON Perhaps we should empty the bucket though – just in case someone kicks it over?

JEAN Now, who's going to kick it over?

Pause. A chuckle; it's inconceivable of course.

Until they all look at RONA. *She is wrestling violently with her empty handbag, angry it hasn't yielded any cigarettes.*

RONA Bollocks to your fag then. I'm going down the bar – bum one off one of the boys.

RONA *kicks her chair and marches out towards the bucket.* SIAN *lunges forward and moves the bucket just in time.* RONA *exits.*

Pause. Relief.

JEAN *moves over to the make-up table and looks at some of the colours. And, with* JEAN's *back turned,* SIAN *hands* MARILYN *the remaining cup of tea.*

JEAN *has spotted one eyeshadow in particular.*

JEAN Oh, now I do like that colour...

REVLON Do you want to try it on?

JEAN Oh no, no – it's not really my kind of thing. I only wear a little powder—

REVLON Some lipstick then? Just to brighten you up.

JEAN And how will it do that, dear?

REVLON *is put firmly in her place.*

That really is a lovely colour though. Where have I seen it before...?

JEAN *takes a little of the eyeshadow and rubs it onto the back of her hand to inspect it closely.*

Meanwhile SIAN *distracts* REVLON.

SIAN So how'd you get into this kind of work?

REVLON I've always loved make-up; ever since I was a little girl.

SIAN Was your mother very beautiful?

REVLON She would have said she knew how to make the best of what she'd been given. She'd never leave the house without "putting her face on" first. She wouldn't be caught dead—

SIAN Looking like us?

REVLON *(agreeing)* No.

(then quickly) Sorry, I don't mean "no". I mean "yes".

(then realising) No, not "yes", I mean...

(then, getting a hold of herself) She was a very proud lady, you know?

A beat. They understand.

SIAN Do you travel around a lot?

JEAN Gloucester! That's where I've seen this colour before. It's almost exactly the same one as the jumper I got Kevin for his school trip to Gloucester. Now there's someone who would have travelled. He loved going away with the school. Loved going anywhere. He couldn't have stayed round here. Well let's face it: prospects round here simply aren't as good for a boy that bright. He'd have had to go away – to study. I doubt I would have seen much of him; I'd have been one of those mothers who complains they never see their sons but it would have been worth it just to see him go and make something of himself. He had such a pleasant manner, didn't he, Sian?

SIAN Proper gentleman.

JEAN He was. A gentleman and a scholar. My husband thinks he would have gone into engineering but I think he would have become a doctor. A surgeon most likely. Course it would have been a struggle to pay for it but now—

She stops herself. Then she realises the others are looking at her.

I was going to say: but *now* with the compensation we could afford to send him wherever he wanted to go.

SIAN You can send Ruth now – give her the chance.

JEAN Oh no – she won't go anywhere, that one. She isn't as clever. I try: I say to her, "Do your homework now like Kevin used to – maybe you'll be as clever as him then." But no, she's not interested. She'd rather pester me. And she was like that before the disaster. In fact, the day it happened she was out with me shopping because she said she was ill. I sent her out to play the other day and she came back moaning that there was no one to play with anymore. I told her straight: "At least you're able to go out to play." That shut her up for a bit.

(then)

She's always rummaging through Kevin's stuff. Playing with his toys and what not. Kevin was such a good boy. Would do what he was told. Such a good boy. So clever. So polite...

REVLON How old is she?

JEAN Who – Ruth? *(then)* Eight.

REVLON She must miss her brother very much.

JEAN I doubt she feels any worse than I do.

REVLON *is struck by the comment and finds it difficult to be near* **JEAN** *for the moment. She quietly moves away.*

JEAN *does not notice. She's too busy admiring the eyeshadow smudged onto the back of her hand. For a moment she enjoys the memory of her son...*

Yes, this is almost exactly the same colour as that jumper I got him...

Then the memory turns painful and bitter. But **JEAN** *controls herself and buries the emotion by rubbing the back of her hand and wiping the colour away.*

RONA *strides back in.*

RONA Awright! Give me that fag.

MARILYN No.

RONA Give it me!

MARILYN No.

REVLON Didn't anyone have any downstairs?

RONA No. Bloody bar is empty. They've all fucked off to join some choir. A choir? What the hell are that lot going to do in a choir?!

JEAN Oh for heaven's sake, have one of mine.

RONA *(to* REVLON *about* MARILYN*)* Do you know how many fags I've given her over the years?

SIAN *(to* REVLON*)* I'll bet you any money she knows the exact figure.

RONA Three thousand! And how many has she given me? *Two!*

MARILYN It's my last one.

RONA So? I've given you my last one before.

MARILYN This is different.

RONA How?

MARILYN It just is.

RONA Alright then, let's share it.

MARILYN No.

RONA Marilyn!!!

MARILYN I'm not smoking it. Nobody's smoking it. It's bad luck.

RONA What?

MARILYN It is – it's bad luck. It's an omen.

RONA What the hell is this now...?

REVLON How do you mean, "it's an omen", Marilyn?

MARILYN The night before the slip, I had one cigarette left and I smoked it after the girls had gone to bed. In the morning I left them at the corner and went to buy some more...

REVLON And then the tip came down?

MARILYN *nods.*

JEAN Marilyn – that had nothing to do with it.

MARILYN The medium said that these things are omens. She said we shouldn't ignore the signs and we shouldn't tempt fate.

RONA Well then all the more reason you should give me that fag. I'll smoke it and break the fucking curse or whatever it is.

JEAN This is why she should come to church.

RONA Does Ken know you talk like this?

MARILYN No – it upsets him.

RONA And do you know why – because it's bullshit!

MARILYN No, it isn't. There's a lot to it. The medium said to look at the facts and the numbers. Like it's a fact it happened on the 21st of October. October is the tenth month. Nineteen sixty-six is the year. So, if you add 21 to 10 to 19 to 66 you get one hundred and sixteen. That's the exact number of children who died.

JEAN She has to come to church. She has to pray.

RONA What – no she doesn't.

MARILYN And the medium said she can reach people.

JEAN (genuinely concerned) Look, Marilyn – these people – they just want your money.

RONA Oh yeah, like the Church never wants your money.

JEAN It's not the same and you know it.

MARILYN The medium says she never asks for money.

JEAN Come to church – pray with us – listen to Billy speak.

RONA She doesn't want to, Jean.

JEAN Alright – but she can still pray because—

RONA Oh Jesus, don't start quoting from the Bible now.

JEAN I wasn't. I was going to say that she can still pray because praying is better than going to this medium.

RONA Is it?

JEAN Of course it is, but you don't understand that because you never have.

RONA Alright then – what do you think she'd pray for? What do you think we'd all pray for? Do you think any of those prayers will be answered. Is He going to send them all back?

JEAN *(indignant, angry)* It is not for you to question God. It is not for *any* of us to question Him. *Or* His purpose. "Many are the plans in a person's heart but it is the Lord's purpose that prevails."

RONA Here we go – it's like listening to Billy now.

JEAN *(angry)* I feel sorry for you. I do. I feel sorry for you because you believe that there's nothing more. That this is all there is.

RONA I'll tell you what I believe: I believe that everything that happens, happens here on earth. But, if there is anyone up there, He certainly works in mysterious ways.

JEAN *(rage!)* Don't you dare; don't you fuck— *(ing)*

JEAN *stops abruptly – remembering herself. However the shock in the room is palpable.*

RONA *(almost taunting* JEAN*)* Christ, were you going to swear just then?

JEAN I'm warning you, *don't* – not about this.

RONA About what?

JEAN You know what.

RONA I don't – what?

JEAN Yes you do. And I'm warning you – don't – or else.

RONA Or else what?

JEAN You know what.

RONA What – you're gonna sort me out?

JEAN Done it before.

RONA When?

JEAN Before.

RONA When?!

JEAN Mr Davies's class.

RONA Mr Davies's class?

JEAN Yes.

RONA We were *twelve* in Mr Davies's class!

JEAN I know that. And you said something to me in History and then later I had you.

RONA No you didn't.

JEAN Yes I did.

RONA When?

JEAN Playtime. I had you by the hair and you were crying because you'd scraped the back of your legs on the stingies and there was a hole in your petticoat.

RONA I don't remember that.

JEAN You don't?

RONA No.

JEAN You remember, Marilyn?

MARILYN Yes.

JEAN You remember me doing all that?

MARILYN Yes.

JEAN *(to* RONA*)* Right? So there!

Pause. JEAN *is satisfied that* RONA *has been put in her place. A few beats and then* MARILYN *leans in.*

MARILYN *(quietly to* JEAN*)* It wasn't her.

JEAN What?

MARILYN It wasn't Rona. *(beat)* It was Jackie Burder.

JEAN It wasn't Jackie Burder. It couldn't have been Jackie Burder. Oh God, it was Jackie Burder.

RONA I knew it wasn't me.

JEAN Oh no.

RONA I never wore a petticoat.

JEAN Wait! Jackie Burder?

MARILYN Yes.

JEAN *Jackie* Burder?

MARILYN Yes.

JEAN Jackie Who's-Downstairs-Working-the-Bar Burder?

MARILYN Yes.

JEAN Oh Jesus.

RONA What?

JEAN How am I going to look at her now?

SIAN Oh come on, Jean, you were twelve.

JEAN That doesn't matter. She comes to church. She does the flowers. *(then)* She does my ironing!

RONA Ha! I knew it!

JEAN Don't start – it's not funny.

MARILYN Oh, it is a bit.

RONA A bit my arse. It's fucking hilarious.

They're all laughing – even JEAN.

I think I will have one of your fags now, Jean.

JEAN *gives* RONA *her cigarettes so she can help herself.*

Here you go, Marilyn, you don't have to smoke your last one now.

MARILYN *(grateful)* I'll keep it for after.

RONA's *about to light up when:*

REVLON Actually, can you not smoke it in here?

RONA What?

REVLON I'm going to fragrance the room in a moment and I don't want it tainted by the smell of cigarette smoke.

RONA What with are you going to fragrance the room may I ask?

REVLON Eau de Parfum – it's what we do.

(to JEAN *suddenly)* Unless you don't want me to?

Pause. The mood in the rooom suddenly changes.

JEAN Why wouldn't I?

REVLON Well, some women don't like strong smells when they're expecting, do they?

Suddenly, a sharp chill descends.

JEAN No. It's fine. You fragrance the room as much as you want.

Clearly REVLON *has hit a herve. There's a very awkward pause.*

RONA Well I'm not going back down the bar – I'll have it on the landing. So don't talk about me, I can hear everything.

RONA *exits.* JEAN *gets up to clear the tea things, making a point of not looking at* REVLON.

JEAN *(brittle)* I'd better take these back down now that we've finished with them. *(then, tersely)* The water's still coming in, Sian.

JEAN *doesn't wait for an answer and exits with the tea things.*

Clearly REVLON *has caused offence and she knows it. Feeling a little exposed, she sprays the room with perfume.*

Both MARILYN *and* SIAN *watch and then breathe in the fragrance (it's almost comforting).*

SIAN Oh that's lovely...

SIAN *sees how wretched* REVLON *feels.*

(to REVLON*)* It's not you. She's the same with everyone. Makes no sense to me but she never mentions the baby. Hates it if anyone else does. So, best not to. Least not in front of Jean.

REVLON *nods (but it doesn't make her feel any better).*

Can I ask you something?

REVLON Of course.

SIAN Who did you call earlier?

REVLON My boss.

SIAN Were you trying to back out of this?

REVLON Yes. But I was told that if I valued my job...

SIAN *nods – understanding fully.*

SIAN Then I suppose we're all stuck here, one way or another.

RONA *enters – hitting the perfume. She finds it overpowering (and shows it) but soon goes over to have a look at* REVLON's *make-up table.*

REVLON *(to* SIAN*)* Why don't we try those eyeshadows on you?

SIAN Oh I don't know, which one would suit me?

REVLON Well, let's have a look. "Let's show the world what exciting eyes and ideas you have."

SIAN What's that?

REVLON Haven't you seen the advert? "Subtle today, bolder tomorrow – bewitching next Tuesday".

RONA Hey, Revlon? What's this stuff?

REVLON *bristles at being called "Revlon".*

REVLON That's Beyond Tanning – the new self-tanning lotion.

RONA *tries quite a large amount on the back of her hand.*

RONA I can't see any difference.

REVLON Be careful—

RONA Why, because it's expensive?

REVLON No. I was going to say it's—

RONA Because I can afford it, if that's what you're worried about.

REVLON Actually, you know what, help yourself.

RONA I will. And I shall be in the Ladies.

She leaves. **SIAN** *and* **REVLON** *exchange a knowing look.*

SIAN I like your lipstick.

REVLON Thank you.

SIAN Could you pick one out for me?

REVLON Oh, I'd love to.

She picks one.

It's a classic: "Cherries in the Snow": "Who knows who you really are? Does he? Who knows the secret hopes that warm your heart. Who knows the dreams you dream. Who knows you sometimes long to sleep in pure-silk sheets…"

SIAN Ooh – Ow!

REVLON You okay?

SIAN Yes – something in my eye. Ow!

REVLON Let me see…

She has a look.

Yeah, it's a lash.

REVLON *retrieves a tissues and gently removes the lash and hands* SIAN *a mirror.*

SIAN Thanks.

SIAN *checks her eye in the mirror and takes a moment to look at her tired face.*

I used to wear make-up all the time. My husband used to say I had the prettiest eyes.

REVLON Well why don't we start with them?

SIAN *readies herself in the chair and closes her eyes.* REVLON *applies the eyeshadow.*

SIAN Every Friday night I'd do this. Every Friday night I'd doll myself up – meet David on the corner – and then we'd go dancing.

REVLON Yeah?

SIAN Yeah, David loved dancing. Absolutely loved it. Some of the boys used to make fun of him – all they wanted to do was drink – but David didn't give a monkey's. He loved spinning me around the dancefloor until I was so breathless I'd almost pass out.

REVLON How long have you been married?

SIAN Nine years.

REVLON And what does David do?

SIAN A miner – what else? All the girls marry a miner.

REVLON Except Jean.

SIAN Except Jean. She married the vicar.

(*then, mindful of* MARILYN) I don't really know Billy. To be honest, he scares me. He's very – um – what's the word?

MARILYN Scary.

SIAN Strong-willed. Looks right at you, you know? He carries a lot of weight round here – just about everyone looks up to him.

MARILYN Not everyone.

Pause. Clearly MARILYN *is one of the few who don't look up to Billy.* REVLON *tries to be the diplomat.*

REVLON Well, I suppose he'd have to be strong-willed. Especially if you're going to carry on believing in God. Look at Jean – she certainly hasn't lost any of her faith.

JEAN *appears, unseen by the others, already overhearing.*

But then again, we all need something to cling to...

(then) But it's odd she doesn't mention the baby. I wonder if she wants another little boy? Or whether she—

JEAN *enters fully catching everyone by surprise. Clearly she's overheard and* REVLON *and* SIAN *are mortified.*

JEAN Sorry. Just came back for my cigarettes. *(then, as she's leaving)* You can carry on now...

JEAN *exits, leaving everyone to hold their breath and bite their tongues.*

REVLON *is clearly shaken and looks at the others.*

REVLON I suppose I should be grateful I wasn't struck down by lightning.

SIAN *smiles. Then, a soft but threatening rumble of thunder from above.* MARILYN, SIAN *and* REVLON *look up worriedly at the skylight.*

MARILYN That was a bit close though.

It breaks the tension. SIAN*'s amused.* REVLON *exhales with a chortle. She composes herself.*

REVLON *(to* SIAN*)* So...

(finding where they left off) You got married nine years ago?

SIAN Yeah.

(then, softly, secretly) And can I tell you a secret? We got married because I fell pregnant with Paul.

REVLON Must have been all that spinning on the dancefloor?

SIAN It was. We were very naughty.

REVLON What did your parents say?

SIAN My father went nuts. And of course he and David worked underground together, so you can imagine.

REVLON But your father came around?

SIAN Eventually. Sort of. Very proper, my father. Like: "Men go out to work, women look after the children". So if David got Paul's bath, or put him to bed, my father would say something. Or if he saw David taking Paul to school or to the dentist's, my father'd have a little dig. And when he found out that David took Paul for things like haircuts and new clothes – and I admit I don't know many men who do that...

REVLON I don't know any!

SIAN No, but my father thought that that was just odd. And he made fun of David a lot over that – called him all kinds of names – especially in front of the other men. But my husband's a tough bloke – he can handle himself – and one day he turned round and told them all straight: no boy of his was going to look like a filthy miner's son, so they could all just – well – I won't swear.

(then, indignant) David just loved his son, that's all. There's nothing wrong with that, is there?

REVLON Nothing at all.

SIAN *(now really defending her husband)* Do you know, he was the first up from the colliery after the tip came down? He'd been off the week before and taken Paul to buy new shoes.

Very smart they were too. Beautiful brown leather. Not like school shoes at all really. And it was David's first day back and he was underground when the alarm was raised. The men came with what they had: a bucket, a shovel, a pick; some had nothing at all. And David – he ran all the way. He didn't stop. And he saw how the slurry had got into the school. He ran around looking for Paul's classroom and somehow got in through a window – and then he started to dig.

(A beat) First he got out the kids who were trapped. Then he got out the ones who were buried but lucky to be alive. But then he started finding the ones who weren't so lucky. But he couldn't find Paul. So he kept digging – finding more bodies; and the men would take them and lay them out in a row, under a blanket – and wait for them to be identified; but still no Paul. So David carried on. He didn't stop, didn't rest, he kept going until his strength gave in and he had to be pulled out. And it was then – when David was getting his breath back, he saw – sticking out from underneath a blanket – Paul's new shoes. Not a mark on them. They'd found Paul on the other side of the school...

(then) David had been digging in the wrong classroom.

(pause) He's a tough man, my husband. All the men are. They have to be, they work underground. They're miners and they're tough. But nobody's that tough. And why should they be? I've seen Marilyn's husband up at the graves, sobbing. Tears streaming down his face. He doesn't care. Nobody does.

(then) David didn't cry. Not even at the funeral. They dug this long trench and placed the little coffins side by side. It was bitterly cold. You could barely hear the prayers. And still he didn't cry.

(then) Except once, weeks later...

(she steels herself) I'd been out shopping and I came back and I heard him. He was in the front room. I went in and there he was, bent over – literally doubled up in the chair

– weeping. I put my hand on his shoulder – just to comfort him like – and he leapt up – as if I'd caught him doing something wrong. He just stared at me. Terrified. He went out and didn't come back for hours. We've never spoken about it since and he can barely look at me now.

(then, lost in her despair) It should have been something we went through together, you know? I go to bed alone and I wake up alone. I can't remember the last time he sat next to me or put his hand on mine. I'd just like him to look at me. You know? Hold my hand... And who knows maybe – one day – go dancing again.

(then, to **REVLON***)* Can I try that lipstick now?

REVLON Yes of course, let me...

REVLON *retrieves the lipstick and goes to apply it...*

SIAN It's okay, I can do it.

REVLON *hands her the lipstick and a mirror.*

Will you tell me that advert again?

Beat. **SIAN**, *with her hands shaking and her emotions rising, puts on the lipstick as* **REVLON** *– her voice unsteady – repeats the advert; its meaning very different from before.*

REVLON "Who knows who you really are? Does he? Who knows the secret hopes that warm your heart. Who knows the dreams you dream. Who knows you sometimes long to sleep in pure-silk sheets..."

SIAN *(tears stinging her eyes)* Yeah, that's the one.

SIAN's *reflection becomes too much for her to bear. She breaks down, desperate to hide it somehow.*

There's that bloody eyelash again!

(then) Sorry, shouldn't swear.

REVLON *gets another tissue for* **SIAN** *as* **JEAN** *returns.*

JEAN Oh that colour's all wrong for you, Sian. It's far too bright—

SIAN *hides her face from* JEAN.

REVLON I think it really suits her.

JEAN I'm sure you know best. You're the expert. *(then)* Oh for heaven's sake, Sian, the water's still coming in.

SIAN Oh, Jean – where's the panic? I've told them and they said they'll do something about it. But it's only a little bit of water. What's the worst that's going to happen...?

A moment. They all know what the worst thing that happens because of a little water is.

You're right. Sorry. I'll tell them again.

She exits with the bucket. Pause.

REVLON *turns away and busies herself;* MARILYN *remains quiet. It is* JEAN *who breaks the awkward silence.*

JEAN Where's Rona?

REVLON In the Ladies.

Pause.

JEAN *(to* MARILYN, *privately)* You know she's leaving the village.

MARILYN No.

JEAN Yeah. Her husband's put in for a transfer to Nottingham. I'm not supposed to know, but Billy told me. They've been up there a couple of times, looking for houses.

MARILYN But she can't. She can't leave.

JEAN Well she is.

MARILYN Well she can't.

JEAN She's got enough money now, so there's nothing to stop her.

Pause. JEAN *realises that she and* MARILYN *are effectively, for the first time, alone together.*

I know why you won't come and hear Billy speak.

A beat. **MARILYN** *is unforgiving.*

MARILYN He had no right. They were *my* children. *Mine.*

JEAN I know. I do. I—

She stops, realising **REVLON** *is nearby – and she's come over to patch things up – and* **JEAN** *very much resents the interruption.*

REVLON Do you want to try some powder now?

JEAN No.

REVLON What about Ruth? Would she like something?

JEAN She gets enough presents, thank you.

REVLON Look, about earlier on when you overheard me talking to Sian—

JEAN If you want to ask me, just ask me.

REVLON Sorry?

JEAN If you want to ask me, just ask me.

REVLON I don't know what—

JEAN Am I having this child to replace Kevin?

(then) That's what you want to know, isn't it? That's what you were thinking when you asked Sian: "would she like another little boy?" It's alright – I doubt you're the first.

REVLON *can't deny it.*

Nothing – will ever – can ever – replace Kevin. Nothing. Not now. Not ever. And *this*; this wasn't planned. It must have happened a few days before the disaster, perhaps even the night before. God saw fit to give me a child, only to take another. It's almost funny, isn't it? I didn't want this one. I wanted the one I had.

Then **JEAN** *becomes mindful of* **MARILYN**.

But when *I* asked what right God had to take my son...

(looking at **MARILYN***)* ...to take all our children...

(then, back to **REVLON***)* ...my husband put me straight: he said Kevin didn't belong to me – they didn't belong to any of us; they belonged to God. We were merely caring for them. So I was not to blame God. I was not to question why He wanted Kevin by his side? Certainly not a boy like that. Certainly not a boy like him.

MARILYN *is watching* **JEAN.**

And the reason why my husband – and I – still *"cling"* to God: why we still believe? For Billy it's in Romans: "And we know that in all things God works for the good of those who love him, who have been called according to his purpose".

It's getting harder now.

And for me? It means that one day *I will* see Kevin again. After all this has passed. After all this is done with, I'll see him again.

(then) And he'll be just the same. He won't have aged, he'll be exactly as he was. And he'll see me, and he'll come to me and know that the time we've been apart will have been nothing – it'll have been no time at all – because from that moment on we'll be together forever. For all time...

(then) Does that answer your question?

REVLON Yes.

Pause. **SIAN** *enters with the empty bucket, unaware of what's transpired.*

SIAN Do not laugh.

JEAN What's that, Sian?

SIAN Don't laugh. I'm serious. Whatever you do. Do-not-laugh.

RONA *(offstage)* The lights in the Ladies are shit – you can't see a bloody thing.

RONA *enters – holding the bottle of Beyond Tanning –
dark fake tan on her face.*

(to REVLON*)* Oi! And this stuff must be defective.

REVLON Well I've got to say it: that really is Beyond Tanning.

RONA What?

SIAN Either that or Shirley Bassey's just walked in.

Now even JEAN *is laughing.*

RONA What the hell is wrong with you?

REVLON *hands her a mirror.*

CHRIST, I LOOK LIKE EARTHA FUCKING KITT!

Laughter breaks out.

REVLON Okay, calm down – it hasn't dried completely, I don't
think.

RONA Get it off, get it off – I look like I've been underground,
for Christ's sake.

REVLON Well I did warn you.

RONA But you let me carry on, didn't you?!

MARILYN Are you really leaving the village?

RONA What?

MARILYN Are you really leaving the village?

RONA Who told you?

MARILYN *looks at* JEAN.

JEAN *Marilyn!*

RONA *(to* JEAN*)* This is you, isn't it? This is you and your
husband. He can't keep his mouth shut either. Unless it's
about swimming pools.

MARILYN She can't leave. She has to stay.

RONA I don't have to do fuck all.

　　(to REVLON*)* Is it off?

REVLON Give me a second.

MARILYN Why are you leaving?

RONA Because I am, that's why! Hurry up, Revlon – get this crap off my face.

REVLON Hey, my name's not Revlon, okay?

RONA This was such a stupid idea, Sian.

　　RONA *grabs a tissue and wipes the fake tan from her face.*

SIAN What? No it wasn't.

RONA Why we let you talk us into it I'll never know. It's so fucking pointless. It's just lipstick!

REVLON Rona, I understand – you're upset – but it's not just lipstick.

RONA What did you just say?

REVLON When?

RONA Just then.

REVLON I didn't say anything.

RONA Yes you did, you said, "I understand."

REVLON No I didn't.

SIAN She didn't, Rona.

RONA I heard her. She said, "I understand."

REVLON I said I understand you're upset—

RONA You understand I'm *upset*?!

JEAN Rona, no!

RONA Do you have children?

REVLON No.

RONA DO YOU HAVE CHILDREN?

REVLON No.

RONA Then you understand *nothing*! All you understand is driving your nice car, seeing us on your nice television and sending us your six poxy shillings.

REVLON *goes to find her purse.*

REVLON Here! Whatever I've got you can have.

SIAN No, don't you dare.

RONA Let her if she wants.

JEAN Rona – stop it!

REVLON I've got a ten bob note and a tanner.

JEAN What is it with you and money? All the time. I'm sick of it.

RONA Oh like you're any different. You like to sit on committees and decide what people can and can't have. You people suit yourselves anyway.

SIAN But it isn't all about money.

RONA Of course it's all about money. It's all it's ever been about. The coal, the tips – everything was about money. Why do you think they dug down for coal in the first place? Money. When anyone wants to dig underneath your house it's because they want to make money. Why do you think the tips are up there on the mountain? Because it was cheaper to do that than to put them underground. That and nobody gave a shit about us.

(to **REVLON***)* When we complained about the flooding they threatened our pay packets. Said that to do anything about it would make the pit unprofitable. Even the Union rolled over on that one.

(then) So what do they do? They keep going. Put seven of them on top of a mountain right above a *fucking school*!

And now when we say we want the other tips cleared, what do they say – it'll cost too much money.

(to JEAN*)* Put up a memorial if you like. In forty or fifty years nobody's going to remember what happened here anyway. It'll be something else by then – another disaster waiting to happen. But it'll be the same people who'll say there's nothing to worry about. The same ones who'll be far away and who'll stand to make a lot of money.

(turning to SIAN *and to leave)* Don't tell me it's not about money. It's always about money.

SIAN But money won't bring your boy back!

RONA *stops.*

The rain has stopped now and it's deathly silent.

RONA *turns to face* SIAN.

RONA *Don't you think I know that?!* But it's all those bastards have got. So I want it. I want their money. I want their money for my boy!

(then) You make fun of me because I won't stand in a queue. Neither should you – not any of you.

(to REVLON*)* We queued outside the chapel – afraid we'd lose our place – waiting all night to identify the bodies. Letting us in one at a time. Taking us along the aisle to see the children laid out on the pews – covered in blankets.

(then) I had dug with my hands until I was dragged off and then they made me wait.

(then) So no, I won't ever queue for anything. I'll never wait to be tapped on the head and told that I'm a good little girl for waiting my turn. Never again.

(then) And the reason I want to leave this place is because I'm sick of being surrounded by women like you. I'm sick of walking down the street and seeing myself.

(then) I'm not like you. I don't want to get involved with committees; or help out and cheer people up; or stand on my front doorstep looking up at the tips.

MARILYN I don't do that.

RONA Yes you do, you do it every day!

Beat.

MARILYN I'm waiting for my children to come home.

RONA They're not coming home. None of them are.

MARILYN They might. One day.

RONA They won't.

MARILYN There were warnings. And still I sent them to school.

RONA I know darling. We all did.

(then, to **REVLON***)* See? No matter how much of this paint we put on, we'll all be the same underneath.

Pause. It sinks in. **REVLON***'s defeated.*

REVLON I think we better call it a night.

JEAN, MARILYN *and* **RONA** *begin to gather up their things.*

SIAN No.

JEAN Maybe we should, Sian.

SIAN But we're not finished.

RONA Yes we are.

SIAN No, come on, please, stay.

REVLON Sorry, Sian.

SIAN What will we tell everyone?

REVLON Tell them I made a mistake.

JEAN We'll say there was a mix-up.

SIAN But it isn't a mix-up. It isn't a mistake.

REVLON Look, Sian, maybe it's not the right time.

SIAN Yes it is the right time. It's exactly the right time. I want to go home tonight, walk in through the door and for my husband to look at me. To *see* me. I want him to *touch* me.

RONA Oh luv, you're better off when they're leaving you alone—

SIAN I WANT ANOTHER CHILD, YOU FUCKING IDIOT!.

(then) I want what she has.

SIAN *is pointing at* **JEAN**.

I don't want money; I don't want to move away; I don't want anything.

(then) I want another baby. And this one I'll love harder than the last – if that's even possible.

(then) I just want to go on. I just want David to hold my hand and for us to go on. I want to give him back what he's lost. And I can do it – I know I can – but first he has to touch me. So I have to be beautiful again.

(then, to **REVLON***)* So you'd better bring that case back in, sit your bony arse down and show me *how*—

SIAN *grabs the vanity case; it opens and make-up spills all over the floor.*

Oh God, I'm so sorry. Sorry, sorry.

REVLON It's okay.

SIAN I didn't mean to do that. I'm so sorry—

JEAN *(to* **SIAN***)* It's alright Sian, it doesn't matter.

SIAN *(to* **REVLON***)* ...please don't go...please don't.

RONA Yeah calm down, Sian, for Christ's sake – it's just lipstick!

REVLON IT'S NOT JUST LIPSTICK! Alright? It's just not.

(then) I may not know anything about anything but I do know that.

Everyone's surprised by the strength of this outburst. They're almost startled. Even **RONA** *– but her instinct is to bite back. Anticipating it,* **REVLON** *shuts her up with:*

(to **RONA***)* My mother lost a child; my father too.

(then) They had a little boy once; and he went to school one day and never came home.

Pause. A big one.

Weary and upset, **REVLON** *picks up the lipsticks from the floor. She has said the one thing she didn't want to say, and is already regretting it.*

The others watch and exchange tired, culpable looks. Even **RONA** *is exhausted now and she sits.*

REVLON *gathers most of the lipsticks and places them back in her vanity case. She zips up the case and turns to leave, only to find* **MARILYN** *in her way – holding one last lipstick.*

MARILYN *hands it to her and sits. She at least would like to hear the story.*

And, as **REVLON** *looks around the room, all the others are sitting and waiting too.*

Nothing earth-shattering. Nothing unique. He drowned. On a school trip, as a matter of fact. They went to a reservoir to see a dam working, and my brother was messing about, and he went in.

SIAN How old was he?

REVLON Ten.

MARILYN How old were you?

REVLON Me? I was eight.

MARILYN *looks instinctively at* **JEAN.**

I was home with my mother when the police arrived. They waited with us until my father came home and then we drove to the hospital. He wouldn't go in so I waited with him in the car. After a while my mother came out and, straight away, I could see she was hiding her face behind her hand.

(beat) She walked across the car park, got in the car, said something to my father and then we drove home.

(beat) What I remember after that was how quiet the house became. I'd hear crying from their room sometimes but otherwise the house was dead. They kept my brother's room exactly as it was. I wasn't allowed to go in there, or play with his toys. My mother would sit in there for hours by herself. She barely spoke to me. My father made all my meals.

(then) She stopped going out; stopped doing her hair; stopped "putting on her face". She couldn't bear the thought of anyone looking at her, you see. She was ashamed. She felt guilty. She felt she had failed. That's why she hid her face that day at the hospital; why she couldn't look at anyone anymore; why she couldn't look at herself.

(then) I'd catch her staring at me sometimes – when I was playing or something – and I honestly didn't know whether she was loving me or hating me.

(then) And then one day she came in and told me we had to go to the shops and I was to get ready. When I found her, she was in her room, sitting at her dressing table, trying to put on some make-up. She was holding a lipstick but her hand wouldn't stop shaking. She waited and waited but it just wouldn't stop. So I went over, took the lipstick and very carefully I put it on for her. And for the first time in a long time, she looked at me. She looked at me as I put on her make-up and then we went out.

(then) That was the day she decided she wasn't going to hide her face anymore. She missed my brother every single day but that's what she did. On the days she found it hard, I'd do it for her. I would brush her hair and put on her

make-up. I'd find the brightest, reddest lipstick she had. The brighter the better.

(then) And I suppose that's why I came here today. Why I volunteered. I thought I could do the same for you. But it was childish and stupid, and I'm sorry; but it's the one thing I know I can do. In the end, it was all my mother could do.

(then, to **RONA***)* So though it is pointless, though it is just paint – it's not just lipstick.

REVLON *gathers up and leaves.*

RONA Okay well, look – Sian – if it means that much to you...

SIAN What?

JEAN Eh?

RONA Well if it means that much to you, we could carry on; I mean, if you really want.

REVLON *has stopped. Everyone is staring at* **RONA***.*

Well Christ, I don't care. And since when is it up to me anyway? It's up to Revlon.

They all look to **REVLON***. It really is now up to her.*

JEAN It is a bit short notice to cancel.

SIAN Will you stay?

RONA Course she will – she's going to look like an idiot if she says she made a mistake.

REVLON Will I?

RONA I think you will. And there's no point blaming the W.I. or the Red Cross; everyone will have seen your bloody big car by now.

Pause. How can **REVLON** *refuse?*

REVLON Well okay – but I'm going to need a volunteer.

Pause.

RONA You'd better go first, Sian – before the crowds get here.

SIAN Thanks, Rona. I'm sorry I swore.

RONA Ah, Fuck it.

MARILYN *goes to exit.*

JEAN Marilyn? Where are you going?

MARILYN I was thinking of asking Ken to take me to the cemetery.

JEAN Okay, but he's afternoons, isn't he?

MARILYN I'll go tomorrow then.

JEAN Why don't we go? Later on. The two of us.

MARILYN I'd like that.

JEAN Would you?

MARILYN Yes. *(then)* But you have to bring Ruth...

A moment. JEAN *looks over to* REVLON.

JEAN I will.

Then, one by one, they all retake their seats; sitting closer together this time.

RONA So come on then, Revlon, show Sian—

(then) Sorry. What's your name?

REVLON It's Charlotte.

RONA Okay then – Charlotte – what's going to make Sian's fella to do the fandango?

REVLON Well then, ladies – good evening and welcome to the world of Revlon. Where every woman deserves to be beautiful. We have some breath-taking colours to show you and some tips to give you a fresh glow.

Lights begin to fade.

Now earlier on I started with Sian's eyes. I may have to start again but that's okay. We can do that. And your husband's absolutely right by the way – they are very pretty...very pretty indeed...

Fade to black.

Curtain.

ENCORE

*It is the end of the night and the ladies are packing up –
returning the room to its original (empty) state.*

RONA So the big galump's afternoons is he?

JEAN Don't call Ken a big galump.

RONA Why not?

JEAN Because he's not. Ken might be big but he's not a galump.

RONA Big? He's huge. I'm surprised they can get him underground.

JEAN Still, he's not a galump is he Marilyn?

MARILYN He is.

JEAN What?

MARILYN He is. He is a galump.

RONA And she should know – she married him.

MARILYN I did. And he is.

JEAN Well that's no thanks to you. You were always chasing him off.

RONA When?

JEAN In school?

RONA That's because he wouldn't leave her alone.

JEAN That's because he fancied her.

RONA Yeah, but he was too rough.

JEAN Ken's not rough.

MARILYN Yes he is. He is rough.

JEAN But not rough-rough?

MARILYN Oh no, not rough-rough, but he is rough. He pinches me all the time.

JEAN *(intrigued)* Oh!

MARILYN He's done it all our married life. I'm peeling potatoes or something and he starts on me.

    JEAN *leans in to* MARILYN.

JEAN Where does he pinch you?

MARILYN *(confidentially)* In the kitchen.

    (then) It's very distracting.

JEAN I can imagine.

MARILYN I threaten him with the peeling knife – nothing. I throw the iron at him – nothing. And then he comes at me and I tell him – if you don't pack it in, Rona Will Get Your Pants!

SIAN What's "Rona Will Get Your Pants"?

MARILYN She'll get his underpants off him.

SIAN What literally?

MARILYN Yes.

JEAN Oh good lord, I remember now. This one, four foot tall, chasing this big galump – sorry, Ken – chasing Ken behind the boys' toilets. Next thing out she comes with his underpants.

RONA Didn't have to take his trousers off neither.

SIAN Aw poor boy—

MARILYN It's the only thing that stops him when he's in one of those moods.

RONA Well if he starts again, bang on the wall and I'll come in and I'll have them. Don't care how big a galump he is.

JEAN *and* RONA *are the last to leave.* JEAN *hands* RONA *a cigarette by the door.*

JEAN Actually how did you get his pants without taking his trousers off?

RONA *puts her hand on the light switch…*

RONA I won't lie – there is a technique to it.

Blackout.

PROPERTY LIST

Essential stage props:

Eight to twelve folding chairs

A small table for **Revlon**'s make-up

High bar stool or chair

Tea tray, cups and saucers

A zinc bucket and mop

CHARACTER PROPS

REVLON:

Make-up products (cleanser, toner, moisturiser, a range of lipsticks, eye-shadow pallets, a self-tanning lotion and make-up brushes) along with hygiene essentials (such as tissues, cotton wool, etc.), plus a vanity case, leather bound notepad, handbag and umbrella.

SIAN:

A handbag, umbrella/headscarf.

MARILYN:

A handbag, tissue, a cigarette packet containing one cigarette, along with a folded and worn child's drawing.

RONA:

A handbag, tissue, cigarette lighter and an empty packet of cigarettes.

JEAN:

A handbag, umbrella, tissue, a coat that disguises her pregnancy, full packet of (better brand) cigarettes.

LIGHTING/EFFECTS

The play is set on a rainy June evening and therefore a simple warm wash will suffice, with perhaps a special/gobo for the skylight and a hanging practical (i.e. a bare light bulb) being desirable. A thoughtful sound design is recommended, not just because the sound of rain and water has a thematic role but also because the sound of heavier rain hitting the skylight (as specified in the text), along with carefully placed occasional rumbles of thunder, can alter the dynamic to great effect whilst underscoring some of the play's most intense moments.

Accompanying the sound of rain should be a constant – and very real – drip of water coming in from the "skylight" and pooling onto the floor before being caught by the zinc bucket. Though originally accomplished with a specialist piece of equipment, the same effect can be achieved very simply (and cheaply) by using a refillable medical IV bag/drip and hung above the main playing area. Recommend filling it with a discrete quantity of water and set at a rate that allows the IV bag to be empty – and the drip to have stopped, along with the sound of rain – by the time SIAN tells RONA "Money won't bring your boy back!"

THIS
IS
NOT
THE
END

**Visit samuelfrench.co.uk
and discover the best
theatre bookshop
on the internet**

A vast range of plays
Acting and theatre books
Gifts

CPSIA information can be obtained
at www.ICGtesting.com
Printed in the USA
FSHW020558280721
83624FS

9 780573 115226